Paul Hyland was born in Poole, Dorset, and now lives in Cerne Abbas. A poet and travel writer, his books include *The Black Heart* (about Central Africa), *Indian Balm* (India) and *Backwards Out of the Big World* (Portugal). His first book, *Purbeck: The Ingrained Island*, was quickly hailed as a modern classic. It is published by the Dovecote Press, as is his *Wight: Biography of an Island*.

Following page
The interior of St Aldhelm's Chapel, St Aldhelm's Head.

DISCOVER DORSET

ISLE OF PURBECK

PAUL HYLAND

THE DOVECOTE PRESS

A Dartford warbler, still a rare sight on Purbeck.

First published in 1998 by The Dovecote Press Ltd
Stanbridge, Wimborne, Dorset BH21 4JD

ISBN 1 874336 58 X

© Paul Hyland 1998

Paul Hyland has asserted his rights under the Copyright, Designs
and Patent Act 1988 to be identified as author of this work

Series designed by Humphrey Stone

Typeset in Sabon by The Typesetting Bureau
Wimborne, Dorset
Printed and bound by Baskerville Press, Salisbury, Wiltshire

A CIP catalogue record for this book is available
from the British Library

1 3 5 7 9 8 6 4 2

CONTENTS

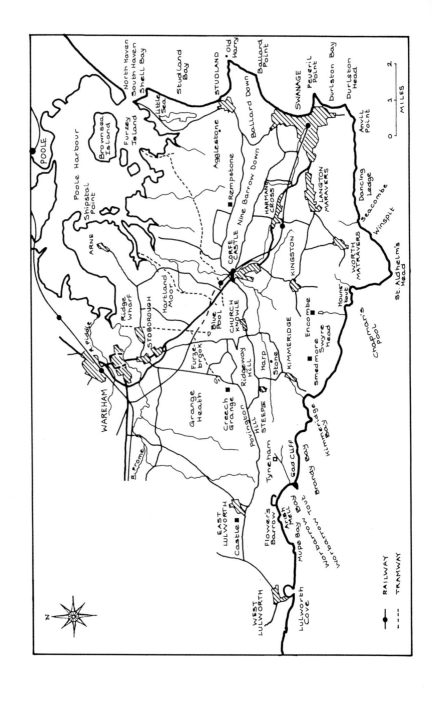

A SIDEWAYS LOOK

If you set sail from Poole for France, out of what anyone will tell you is the second largest natural harbour in the world, you'll see unfolding on your starboard bow the coastline of the little paradise you're missing by not staying at home.

It is called the Isle of Purbeck. Between Poole Harbour's wooded islands you can glimpse its indeterminate north shore: vanished quays, heathy points and secretive inlets which give way, beyond the harbour mouth where the chain ferry runs, to lengths and curves of glorious sandy beach backed by rumpled dunes and tracts of rugged heath. A line of green hills becomes a bleached cliff that stutters into the sea off Handfast Point: white stacks which fascinate as shifting clouds or old bones do, a reflection of the Needles twenty miles east.

Old Harry Rocks and Handfast Point from the deck of a cross-Channel ferry.

Durlston Head and Castle, with the Large Globe set back
from the edge of the cliff.

This is how we look at the raw edge of a place, land's arbitrary
cross-section scoured by waves. Between those stacks – called Old
Harry Rocks – and the bulk of Ballard Down, the Pinnacles stand
before a swelling bastion of chalk. Then Ballard Cliff plunges into
Swanage Bay where the new town squats along the brink of a long
lazy bite that the sea has taken out of colourful clays. The beach
meets Peveril Point's hard stuff and Swanage old town climbs onto a
plateau of limestone. Forbidding faulted strata dip and climb over the
rocky shore of Durlston Bay. High on Durlston Head squat the
turrets and castellations of a mock castle. Deep in the rock face the
Tilly Whim Caves gape, the first of many cliff quarries once hacked
out to build harbours and cities. A dry combe is a deep notch in the
rock's horizon. On Anvil Point a lighthouse winks, winks.

That's what you leave behind as you make out into the Channel. If you look back now, all you can see are massive grey cliffs fortifying Purbeck against whatever storms can throw at it. The armoured coastline runs due west, punctured by more inky caverns, negatives of gleaming buildings erected far away, a litany of names known to stonecutters, fishermen and smugglers: Blackers Hole, Dancing Ledge, Scratch Arse, Smokey Hole, Topmast, Hedbury, Seacombe and Winspit.

There Purbeck drives a great wedge of rock against the sea, against the horizon. Jutting St Aldhelm's Head is topped with a tiny chapel and buoyed up by a skirt of dark clays and shales. Those Kimmeridge Beds are the oldest rocks on Purbeck and hint at a magical landscape hidden beyond the headland. From white sands to grim shales, you've sailed past – and taken a sideways look at – 200-million-years-worth of geology laid down, contorted and crammed into an island of some sixty square miles.

It's that unimaginable time scale concentrated within so small an area, or rather, volume, that gives the coast and the landscapes behind it their remarkable variety. If you travel within the little island – at its longest and widest it's only twelve miles by nine – you pass from one country to another in quick succession, each with its own shapes, colours, rocks, soils, vegetation, crops, raw materials, buildings, occupations; each speaking to you, if you will listen, in its own language, its own rooted discourse, its gossip.

THE ISLAND

Despite its intoxicating variety the island has its own identity, a sense of itself somehow independent of the human creatures who have exploited and cherished it in the latest few moments of its long life. Islands are like that: they have their own air, their own rhythm and pace. But however insular it is, Purbeck is no more an island than, say, the Isle of Dogs or the Isle of Thanet. It is a peninsula washed on two sides by sea, on the third side by the River Frome and Poole Harbour, and on the west side is anciently defined by a stream called Luckford Lake which trickles into the Frome from sources far below Flowers Barrow on the chalk ridge, an Iron Age hillfort whose southern ramparts have fallen away into the sea. It's as if the cartographer's quill ran out of ink and left the island's last edge to our imagination. Purbeck is an island of the mind.

It used to be more literally an island. In the old days marshes extended high up the Frome valley and the green road from Lulworth along the chalk ridge was the one reliable route into Purbeck. Then, two thousand years or so ago, a narrow causeway was built across soggy ground from Wareham, making that settlement Purbeck's gateway until, recently, a bypass unclogged the Saxon walled town and allowed tourist and industrial traffic to pour in and out of the island.

As a child I used to come from home in Parkstone across on the Sandbanks chain ferry. Twenty years ago, when I first wrote about Purbeck, I entered it through Wareham's walls and infallibly found myself possessed by the spirit of the island. Since then I have written books about distant places. Now I have risked returning. The danger in revisiting childhood haunts is that they will seem smaller, less numinous, more prosaic. The likelihood is that time and so-called development will have exorcised their enchantment. I have come back to find that the Isle of Purbeck draws and stirs me just as before. It is as exotic as it ever was, and strangely larger.

So I join the traffic that pours along the Wareham bypass. Pours, that is, until it reaches the gap in the hills plugged by Corfe and its castle. The pressure on the place holds many dangers. Purbeck has survived, and been shaped by, those who have exploited it over many centuries for shale, marble, freestone, chalk, clay and oil. Despite all that, scars become beauty spots and the innocent tourist enthuses over how 'unspoilt' the place is. 'The country here is lovely beyond words', the artist Augustus John wrote to Will Rothenstein. 'Corfe Castle and the neighbourhood would make you mad with painter's cupidity.' But the isle is not invulnerable. While I abhor efforts to pickle it in aspic, to conserve it like an exhibit, to deny its very life, I fear outsiders and insiders who do not value it enough. Most of all I am wary of those who value it, sure enough, but whose cupidity – or simple greed – persuades them to destroy the thing they love.

CASTLES

CORFE

'There is in the Isle of Purbecke a strong castle called Corffe Castle, seated on a very steep hill, in the fracture of a hill, in the very midst of it . . . ', said the *Mercurius Rusticus* in 1643. The castle in the gap was built to withstand unwanted visitors. It is still the island's hub, an icon on a thousand brochures. Many more recognise this ruin's profile than have heard the name of Purbeck. Because the castle in its glory was a potent symbol Cromwell's Parliament passed an Act to slight it. It had withstood two Civil War sieges, defended by Lady Mary Bankes for the king, until the treacherous or pragmatic Lieutenant-Colonel Pittman led Roundheads in instead of Royalist

Lady Mary Bankes holding Corfe
Castle's keys, at Kingston Lacy.

reinforcements and took the castle from within and without with the loss of one life. The icon had to be razed. Sappers undermined gatehouses, walls, towers and the keep itself. A fortune in public money was expended on gunpowder packed in beneath.

Fuses were lit. The charges made a spectacular show. Towers slumped, walls sagged, Henry III's Martyr's Gate was torn in two as one half shuddered and sank six feet lower than the other, King John's gloriette burst and Henry I's keep split like a box. But the strong castle of Purbeck stone could not be levelled. The ruin has stood proud ever since, just as it is.

Well, almost. Wind, rain and frost have scoured and nibbled at it. In 1774 John Wesley noted that a rector of Corfe had for years occupied rooms, fitted with a fireplace, window and other amenities, in the south and north towers. The National Trust, to whom Ralph Bankes left the castle in 1981, has made the greatest change to the fabric in more than 350 years. In the winter of 1995-6 three chunks of fallen masonry were shifted – the largest weighed eighty tons – to re-open the gateway to the inner ward. Now we can enter the shattered keep as of old. The stonework here is stronger than elsewhere, held together by thick pinkish mortar partly composed of burnt clay or crushed brick. When Parliament's gunpowder stunned the King's Tower its mortared joints held and the very stones split.

The oldest masonry is a wall of herringbone work in the west bailey, part of the Old Hall that stood here soon after the Norman Conquest of 1066, and perhaps before it. Earlier rubble, post-holes and pottery lie beneath it and we can imagine the Saxon king Edward visiting his stepbrother at Corfe Gap on 18 March 978. Exhausted from hunting, he craved refreshment. Still on horseback, he took a cup of wine proffered by Ælfryth his stepmother or her chief men. Then he was stabbed, seized and, his left foot trapped in the stirrup, dragged by his horse. Corfe claims the whole embroidered tale: the impulsive young king and the beautiful wicked stepmother who put her own son Ethelred on the throne. The church is dedicated to St Edward, King and Martyr. St Edward's Fountain is supposed to have sprung up by St Edward's Bridge at the foot of Castle Hill to mark his first burial place. Its water cured weak, or credulous, eyes.

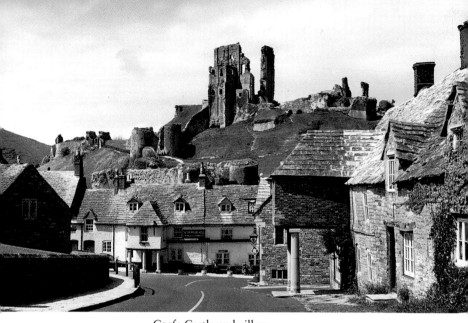

Corfe Castle and village.

Corfe Castle saw treacheries, but never much action. It held many noble prisoners, and more who were tortured, dropped into its dungeon and simply forgotten. It was a symbol of terrifying power. See the fine ruins of its gloriette, but never forget its oubliette. In days when deer were prized more than peasants, it overlooked the royal chase. It oversaw the rich medieval trade in marble that flowed through Corfe Gap. Later, it supervised and profited from smuggling and piracy. It was the axis on which the island spun.

From the sea we looked at Purbeck's edge. From the castle's keep we can look outwards at the island. We too can oversee it, and get a sense of what we're at the heart of. We can marvel at the rivers, now shrunk to streams, that ran inwards and cut through the chalk east and west of Castle Hill instead of running out to sea. We can try to picture geology's flux. Taking E.M. Forster's advice in *Howards End*, we can climb the hills that overshadow the castle: 'If one wanted to show a foreigner England, perhaps the wisest course would be to take him to the final section of the Purbeck hills, and stand him on their summit, a few miles to the east of Corfe. Then system after system of our island would roll together under his feet.'

An eighteenth century view of Lulworth Castle.

LULWORTH

But first, I want to lead you to the western end of the chalk spine, just beyond Purbeck's invisible boundary, to another ruin. As a boy I clambered in Lulworth Castle's overgrown shell. The Weld family house, it had burnt spectacularly in 1929. It is still a shell, but roofed, made safe and partially restored by English Heritage.

Elizabeth I had sold her castle at Corfe to Sir Christopher Hatton, so in 1608 Lord Howard of Bindon began to build Lulworth Castle to compete, not as a fortress but as a grandiose hunting lodge from which, seven years later, James I would ride out, the last monarch to hunt in Purbeck chase. In 1641 Lulworth was sold to Humphrey Weld, of a Catholic family of grocers who traced their line back to Edric the Wild in King Ethelred's reign. Soon requisitioned as a Royalist garrison, Weld's castle was taken by Parliament in 1644.

Pillaged then, it later underwent intermittent structural changes and refurbishments until, in 1926, *Country Life* celebrated it in a sumptuous feature. Then an electrical fault gutted it. Now we can climb the south-east tower on a metal stair up through the ghosts of former rooms. The vaulted basement – kitchen, wine cellar, servants' hall and so on – contains re-used stones and a doorway from Bindon

Abbey. Above it, a patchwork fabric of blocked arches, suspended fireplaces, beam sockets, pegs and relict plaster hint at the building's metamorphoses, harking back to a medieval-style hall and forward to eighteenth-century symmetries. Notes and *Country Life* photographs on display allow us cheaply to restore the castle – billiard room, King's room, saloon, chapel and all – to its latest glory in our minds.

The chapel is important, for the Welds' story is not just that of latter-day feudalism. It is a chapter in the story of English Catholicism, of survival despite penalties and persecution. In 1786 Thomas Weld obtained permission to build a chapel in his grounds, or, as George III put it, 'to build a mausoleum and . . .' (we can hear the royal ahem!) ' . . . you may furnish it inside as you like.' On one of his later family outings from Weymouth, the king approved. Fanny Burney called it 'a Pantheon in miniature'. Topped by a dome and lantern, with an extravagant altarpiece by Giacomo Quarenghi who became architect to Catherine the Great of Russia, St Mary's was the first Catholic church to be built in England since the Reformation. Here, in 1790, John Carroll of Maryland was consecrated the first Roman Catholic bishop of North America.

St Mary's, East Lulworth, built disguised as a lodge in the 1780s, but the first Roman Catholic church to be built in England after the Reformation.

Flowers Barrow, an Iron Age hillfort half fallen into the sea.

Seven Trappist monks, exiles from revolutionary France, found a home at Lulworth in 1794. Thomas Weld built for them a monastery dedicated to St Susan. In the next twenty years the community, and suspicion of it, grew. A monk named James Power deserted, threw off his habit, abjured his faith in Blandford parish church and accused his brothers of scandalous practices. Not long afterwards, in 1817, the community of sixty-four sailed from Weymouth for Brittany.

When Charles X arrived at Lulworth in 1830, a refugee from the July revolution with his entourage and his gold, it is said that on seeing the castle he exclaimed, 'Voilà, la Bastille!' During his seven weeks' stay prices of Purbeck produce doubled and trebled.

The view from the top of Lulworth Castle is thought-provoking. Southwards, over the tower of St Andrew's, we gaze down a vanished road that ran from the village – a community clustering around the Anglican church until moved out of sight of the castle in the eighteenth century – to the bay of Arish Mell (Arse Mill) where T.E. Lawrence loved to bathe. There, now, a waste pipeline from Winfrith's atomic reactors runs out to sea between the buttocks of Bindon and Rings Hills, and the whole area lies in the Army's

Lulworth Cove, Stair Hole and the Lulworth Crumple, by J. M. W. Turner.

Lulworth Range. Some moonlit nights, they say, a ghostly Roman legion still marches over Bindon Hill and up Rings Hill to the sharp profile of Flowers Barrow. Frederick Treves (of 'Elephant Man' fame) wrote of that Iron Age fort and Lulworth Castle that 'between the old stronghold and the new is interposed nothing less than the history of the world.' That history includes the ruins of Monastery Farm where Trappist silence is pulverised by gunfire.

Looking eastwards from the castle, we pick out Wareham on the Frome, Poole Harbour, the heath, and Creech Barrow Hill hunched at the northern flank of the Purbeck Hills. Go to Lulworth Cove and climb Dungy Head to see a dramatic cross-section of Purbeck's other half: Chalk, Greensand, Wealden Beds, contorted Purbeck Beds and Portland Stone. Beyond the cove, serrated Gad Cliff is succeeded by Broad Bench's snout and the high points of Swyre Head, Houns-tout and St Aldhelm's Head set against the hungry sea.

The Lulworth Crumple is textbook geology for students. How the great J.M.W. Turner, whose instinct was for drama in landscape and weather, would have enjoyed knowing that the rocks he sketched in 1811 at Stair Hole, where the sea is biting out new coves, were tipped and folded by the very earth movements that raised the Alps.

Lulworth Cove from the east.

For me, Lulworth defines the word 'cove'. A sheltered, prismatic beauty, a limestone gateway entered in the old days by pleasure steamers, a dizzying backdrop of chalk down. Lulworth's safe haven was an Elizabethan buccaneer's dream, where the noblest and humblest Dorset natives involved themselves in piracy, against or together with officers supposed to outlaw it. The same was true of the unromantic underground smuggling economy of the eighteenth century. Lulworth specialised in the illegal export of Dorset-bred horses. Geology, natural history and this unnatural history are all on show in the excellent Heritage Centre, set in a vast car park laid out as if to dramatise the damage tourism does to such delicious places.

A farmer's wife died in 1888 aged 104. She knew French through her father's trade in china and swore that as a girl, prior to Trafalgar, she saw Napoleon himself on foot here with an aide, prospecting for invasion routes. Boney folded his map and spat, 'Impossible!'

INVASIONS

It is hard to imagine the repeated invasion of successive land surfaces by seas, lagoons, lakes, rivers and more seas, the slow accretion of the planet's skin punctuated by traumatic shunts, contortions and inversions. On the coast walk east, when the Army Ranges are open, we discover the Fossil Forest, tufa deposited by algae around trunks of pines and cycads in a fossil soil, the Purbeck

Dirt Bed. In his *Dorset Essays* Llewelyn Powys evokes that lost world with more poetry than science: 'In lagoons filled sometimes with salt water, sometimes with brackish water, sometimes with fresh water, the dinosaurs took their pastime ... Around fern-like growths, palmettos and trees of the coniferæ family, clouds of grey insects quivered and danced; but when the sun uprose from the ocean wastes, beyond where St. Aldhelm's Head now stands, there were no birds with tremulous madrigals to hold the dawn under an enchantment.'

Occupation of the ranges makes the MOD the biggest landlord in Purbeck. Tanks score the terrain with caterpillar tracks and pound it with shells, but the army prevents wholesale invasion of the heath and 'improvement' of chalk grassland by plough, pesticide and artificial fertiliser. It repels caravan sites and houses. The army has conserved by neglect since the 1940s, though recently the policy has

A cycad bole in the Fossil Forest.

A Lulworth skipper butterfly.

grown less passive. The rare Lulworth Skipper butterfly is well suited to unkempt grass on the firing ranges while the Adonis Blue needs the grazed turf of the downs.

Adders, grass snakes and five species of orchid thrive on Bindon Hill with only the intermittent passage of humans to threaten them when the Range Walks are open. Then we can approach Worbarrow Bay the best way, above Smugglers Cave and Mupe Rocks. Think how small a rise in sea level would breach the chalk at Arish Mell. Tides would invade the heath, swell Luckford Lake and flow to meet the River Frome. Purbeck would be a real island at last.

HEARTLANDS

LOST TYNEHAM

Worbarrow Bay is a magical place to watch the sun go down. On one side Flower's Barrow dominates the chalk cliff; on the other Worbarrow Tout stacks Purbeck Beds against a buttress of Portland Stone. Between chalk at Cow Corner and reddish marble at the Tout's foot, Greensand gives way to ochrous Wealden beds and, on the beach, pebbles grade to shingle. Yachts ride an imperceptible swell. If you blink, they might change to fishing boats. Footings on the cliff might stand up as fishermen's cottages, ruins on ancient fields might grow into busy farms, and the whole valley nestling between the hills and Gad Cliff's jagged edge might repopulate itself.

Worbarrow Bay in the 1930s, when today's ruins were cottages.

Tyneham village in the 1920s.

In 1943, a week before Christmas, 225 people faced eviction from 102 Tyneham properties. They pinned a notice on the church door: 'Please treat the church and houses with care; we have given up our homes where many of us lived for generations to help win the war to keep men free. We shall return one day and thank you for treating the village kindly.' A sign planted in the village bore the War Department's pledge: that after US Sherman Tank crews had practised D-Day landings, after the WAAF and RAF had vandalised Tyneham House, old when Celia Fiennes admired it in 1608, after the forces had no further use for this valley, its native inhabitants would have every right to return home. It was an empty promise.

A stream runs in the gwyle whose dense trees were coppiced religiously. Trunks full of shrapnel would stop chain-saws now. A bunker contains an engine which drives a moving target across the valley on hidden rails. In an Edwardian phone kiosk the line is dead. Houses are tidy ruins. The church is a museum. In the touchingly preserved village school, a notice above the stopped clock and the portrait of King George says, 'Lost: Several golden minutes between Sunrise and Sunset. No reward is offered as they are lost forever.' For several minutes, read half a century and counting.

Two views of Tyneham House. The engraving shows it in the nineteenth century, the photograph of the house as a vandalised ruin was taken in 1951.

[23]

The Lawrence-Washington arms in
St Michael's church, Steeple.

STEEPLE'S STARS AND STRIPES

I found hymn books in St Michael's at Steeple inscribed 'Tyneham
Church. 1930. Not to be taken away.' They were. After 1943
Tyneham's organ was also installed here. The church's surroundings
are charming but somehow too spacious. Long before Tyneham was
evacuated, both the hamlet at Lutton in Steeple and Steeple village
itself thinned and disappeared. If you look hard you can find
hollow-ways, house-sites, and a windmill tump near the church.

In 1540 Steeple, and Creech Grange north of the chalk ridge,
were bought by Sir Oliver Lawrence whose family had intermarried
with Washingtons in the fourteenth century. Heraldry tells tales. The
shields of arms on the wagon roof of St Michael's nave show the
Lawrences' *argents cross ragoulé gules* quartering the Washingtons'
argent two bars and in chief three mullets gules, or stars and stripes.
John Washington settled in Virginia in 1657 and his great-grandson
George became first President of the United States.

Bonds bought out Lawrences. After their chapel of St John the Evangelist at Creech Grange was consecrated in 1859, Steeple's curate was obliged to clamber over Grange Hill in all weathers to celebrate communion. They say he spent a summer cutting steps in the chalk to ease his winter duties. Grange Arch, a folly born of delightfully childish megalomania, is sited just over the hill's summit, on the skyline from the point of view of Creech Grange. Denis Bond built his eye-catcher after adding a Palladian south front to the house in 1738. The arch belongs to the National Trust and the steep squint through Great Wood to Creech Grange is not always kept clear.

Walk the green road eastwards and, before Cocknowle quarry's white scar, a saddle of land joins bracken-clad Creech Barrow Hill. 'Creech', from the Celtic *cruc*, means 'hill'. 'Barrow', from the Saxon

Creech Grange, the east front.

Creech Arch.

beourg, is also 'hill'. Creech Barrow Hill is an etymological freak: it means 'hill' three times over. A geological freak too, it is built of the Bagshot Beds that underlie the heaths as far as Poole Harbour, but topped by an outlier of Bembridge limestone which gives it a grassy summit. Up there, amid a strange cross-in-square of banks and ditches, are the footings of a building which tradition assigns to King John, one of three hunting lodges in Purbeck Chase.

BALL CLAYS

Just now I stand on top of Creech Barrow in the early morning. Below me a sea of mist thins and thickens. It gusts between me and the chalk ridge. Patchily the world reveals itself. Eventually I'll see the Isle of Portland, the hills of Devon and Dorset, Bournemouth and the Isle of Wight. For now, flecks of sheep swirl around a farmer's speeding quad-bike. Creech Grange's neo-Gothic east front makes it look quite a different house. Beyond it, Povington's open clay pit on the Army ranges is a massive wound, begun in 1949. English China Clays (ECC) and its predecessors operated there without planning permission for twenty years. It is the most obvious symptom of the ball clay industry that has dominated this area for so long.

An open pit, where vast machines gouge out gorgeous flesh, is impressive, but nothing beats walking a 'roadway' deep in one of the mines. Inclines are sunk into the ball clay that was deposited as lenses in the Bagshot sands and gravels. Mining is by retreat. At a lens's extremity men dig with pneumatic spades and fill wagons that rumble off along the tramway to the surface. Because the blue-grey clay is plastic, it presses downwards, inwards and upwards at once. Pit-prop frames of larch and pine brace the ceiling, walls and floor of the roadway. The smell is clean and resinous.

Creech Barrow's own substance has been mined many times. Buff clay from it fed the Bond family brickworks. Sands were worked in a pit hidden by Cotness Wood. The valuable ball clay was got from inclined mine-shafts in its flanks. Today an incline to the north-west, at Alder Moor, yields a special grade of clay, machinable when fired, used for electrical insulators. The latest mine at Norden, towards Corfe, started production in 1996 of a rare clay for refractory ware.

Miners using pneumatic spades in English China Clays Norden Seven ball clay mine, 90 metres below Creech Barrow and Alder Moor and up to half-a-mile from the surface.

A Pike Brothers clay pit on Creech Heath, 1932.

Clay-working in Purbeck has a long history and prehistory. In recent times – from the seventeenth century onwards – the business has grown in the hands of Hydes, Pikes, Fayles and others who responded first to growing imports of tobacco from Virginia with clay for pipes (pipe-clay is ball clay's other name), and then to the fashion for tea and porcelain from the East with clay for the likes of Josiah Wedgwood to manufacture teapots, cups and saucers.

BLUE POOL

Worked-out pits are backfilled and reseeded where once they were left to flood and stagnate. But, as I have said, scars can become beauty-spots. The pit known as the Blue Pool was dug about 1850. In 1934 it was bought by T.T. Barnard and opened to the public the next year. Miss J.S. Barnard has run it since 1950 and has resisted modernisation. She is right. It is a wonderful tourist attraction of which the most attractive element is still the pool of three acres, forty-odd feet deep. Refraction of light in a colloidal suspension of clay particles turns the water-filled pit into a romantic 'Black Forest' lake. Its turquoise is set in pine woods and walks where badger setts and fox lairs are lovingly marked. On hot sunny days particles settle and the pool is at its greenest. On cold overcast days it is deep blue.

Pike Brothers' rail tramway took the clay due north to be shipped from Ridge Wharf on the Frome. From Norden wagons were drawn, first by horse and then by a succession of locomotives on Fayle's tramway, to Middlebere Quay on Poole Harbour and, later, north-east to Goathorn Pier. Rival tramways were made uniform in gauge when the competitors merged. Then narrow-gauge rails were abandoned altogether in 1970, two years after ECC took over. The old route from Blue Pool to Ridge skirts Furzebrook where clay is shredded, dried, blended and exported from Purbeck on the main-line via Wareham. Tramways are fading scars on the heath's wild face.

LONG VIEWS AND CLOSE SECRETS

KIMMERIDGE CLAY

In 1567, more than a century before Bonds replaced Lawrences as lords of Creech, Steeple Manor House was bought by Clavells whose family acquired Smedmore by marriage in 1427. The portentous folly on Hen Cliff, the Clavel Tower reflected in Kimmeridge Bay, was built by Revd John Richards (aka Clavell) who inherited Smedmore in 1817. When he died intestate his housekeeper forged a will, but the courts found for his niece, Mrs Mansel. Smedmore has not been sold since 1391. The present Mansel opens his house, a Georgian façade with a Jacobean core, and his garden to the public.

Smedmore House, the west front.

Clavel Tower and Hen Cliff, Kimmeridge, with heavy seas
breaking on the Kimmeridge Ledges.

If the ball clays north of the Purbeck Hills are among the youngest deposits, Kimmeridge Clay comprises the island's oldest rocks; from Tyneham Cap to Chapman's Pool it underlies a spectacular but secretive swathe of landscape. Last time I paid to park on the cliffs at Kimmeridge I was faintly shocked to see an ice-cream van. The tide was exceptionally low. The treacherous Kimmeridge Ledges – that whisk the water in rough weather – stretched out like the tines of a fork. Warm haze hung between funereal cliffs above a glazed sea. I sniffed a hint of sulphur in still air. Children prospected for wonders off ledges. The bay is a marine nature reserve. Seal-like figures snorkelled and gazed at an exotic world. Sucking at his melting lolly, a man said, 'Why pay for this? There's nothing here.'

Beyond a toll-hut and an ice-cream van, the Mansels refuse to commercialise the bay. It is Purbeck's good fortune that, by default or design, landowners have not turned it into an amusement park. The man's friend replied, without enthusiasm, 'Unspoilt, isn't it.'

The cliffs show a layer of bituminous shale known as 'blackstone' or 'Kimmeridge coal'. Bangles cut from it by hand were worn by Iron Age skeletons found nearby. Later, flint-tooled lathes turned cups, spindle-whorls and armlets. In the Roman period dishes, trays, plaques and table-legs were carved from it and polished with beeswax till they glowed like jet. Like Purbeck marble, blackstone was exported to many towns, to Silchester and Verulamium.

Cottagers always burned the 'coal' on their hearths. In the 1970s spontaneous combustion turned rocks red on the cliff above Clavell's Hard. Rails run off the clifftop and old tracks zig-zag from adit to disused adit. Caverns in the cliffs were linked by tramway in the last century. William Clavell had an alum works here about 1600. He tried salt-boiling and the manufacture of green drinking glass too, but all his enterprises met with more or less dramatic rebuffs and led to the debtor's prison. Clavell's Pier survived, heavily built in the style of Lyme Regis's Cobb, until it was broken up by high seas in 1745.

Eight nineteenth-century businesses tried to make fortunes from the blackstone. It was distilled and processed into naphtha, varnish, pitch, dyes, grease and paraffin wax. It produced fertiliser or Kimmeridge 'guano'. Gas refined from shale oil was used to light the city of Paris. The shale itself purified London sewage. Stone from Cuddle promontory made the adamantine Medina Hydraulic Cement that went into French military installations at Rochefort and L'Orient and breakwaters at Alderney and Cherbourg.

Signs of past industry are everywhere, but are as hard to decipher as the mysterious mesh of lines chiselled by the sea and inlaid with pale precipitate in Charnel's grim stone shelf. Kimmeridge has been plundered over and over again. And, as the man said, it's unspoilt.

There is an oil well though, on the cliff just this side of the army ranges' boundary. Oil was struck in 1959 and production started the next year. A nodding donkey draws up 100 barrels a day, taken by road tanker to Furzebrook. It is the small beginning of a big story.

A cottage in Kimmeridge.

When I last saw it, the donkey was stock still. There is geological drama of course, relics of bizarre history, an extravagant submarine world. There is a grim beauty, a moody charm about the place, not to mention an ice-cream van and toilets. But, really, as the first man remarked, there is nothing here at all.

We can climb to Purbeck's highest point, Swyre Head, from the quarry car park above Kimmeridge village. (Don't confuse it with the other Swyre Head beyond Lulworth, just west of Durdle Door and Scratchy Bottom.) The walk to it along Smedmore Hill, with land sloping away on our left and dropping steeply on our right, offers views north across the Corfe valley, to Church Knowle and Corfe Castle, and south down to the lush swelling dairy country of the Kimmeridge Clay, to Smedmore House and the Clavel Tower.

'Swyre' comes from the Old English for neck, or beak of a ship. It does look like a vessel's prow or a grassy ziggurat. At 666 feet, it is just 13 feet taller than the summit of the Purbeck hills. From the Bronze Age burial mound that tops this inland headland we can see, on a clear day, Dartmoor in Devon to the west, the Isle of Wight to the east and France – Normandy's Cotentin peninsula – to the south.

ENCOMBE

Now if we make for Kingston but, just before it, turn south for Houns-tout, our route lets us walk around and high above the Golden Bowl, a hill deep within the other-worldly valley in which the private, almost arcane, estate of Encombe lies.

William Culliford grew up down there and, in the late seventeenth century, worked for the Treasury to expose fraud, corruption and smuggling in south-west England and south Wales. The Isle of Purbeck in general, with Brandy Bay and Chapman's Pool so close, must have schooled him well in the vices he would investigate.

In 1734 the Cullifords sold Encombe to the Pitts, who owned Kingston, thus re-uniting manors that once belonged to the Abbey of Shaftesbury. In 1770 John Pitt finished the big house, probably built to his own designs, of white ashlar with colonnades and porticoes beneath a cornice of just the right weight and breadth to settle the building harmoniously within its own amphitheatre.

His son, William Morton Pitt, had a vision for Purbeck and the nation. With William Clavell he drew up plans in 1796, at the height

The Encombe valley.

of the French wars, for the defence of England in the event of invasion. Among his passions was the reform of prisons, asylums and work-houses. He worked for the education of labourers' and fishermen's children. He campaigned for cottagers to have their own smallholdings and he set up industries – rope-making, sailcloth manufacture, straw-plaiting and herring-curing – to employ the poor of Kingston, Langton, Corfe and Swanage and to 'detach them from the pursuit of that illicit traffic which, from the contiguous situation of this place to the sea coast, they had long been able to follow'.

His own idealism and the poor's reported indolence failed him. In 1807 he sold Encombe to John Scott, Lord Chancellor in his cousin William Pitt the Younger's government, later the first Earl of Eldon. Scott was as reactionary as Morton Pitt had been reforming. Son of a coal factor from Newcastle, he rose through the law and in high office opposed Morton Pitt's efforts to procure decent wages for Dorset agricultural labourers. Militia were ready to defend Encombe against riot when the Reform Bill was at first thrown out. He also

Encombe House and lake in the Golden Bowl.

opposed religious liberty, Catholic emancipation, popular education and the 'dangerous innovation' of the Great Western Railway.

One night not long after he bought it a fire raged in the house. John Scott rushed outside to bury the Great Seal for safety. Next day he forgot where he had hidden it. The household were set to digging. It was recovered. The house was refurbished and John Scott and his son added new buildings and improved the park. On the sheep-sprinkled hill above Quarry Wood Lord Eldon had a forty-foot obelisk of freestone quarried at Seacombe erected in honour of his elder brother, Sir William Scott, the Baron Stowell.

Maybe it was the fire that gave the second Earl such a taste for water. Today the pillared Temple opens on to a swimming pool.

Then, the house and its artificial lakes were supplied by an extraordinary and near-invisible feat of engineering. A half-mile tunnel, lined with fine masonry and ventilated by three vertical shafts, was driven through Westhill at a gradient of 1 in 866. With its associated reservoirs, tanks, hydraulic rams and 4,000 yards of cast iron pipe, it brought running water into the dry valley.

It was a promised land flowing with milk and money. More stonework plumbing takes the stream past Encombe Dairy where cattle on the farm road cross a 'rustic' or 'picturesque' bridge of massive Purbeck rocks. The stream runs on down the gwyle and tips a waterfall into the sea off the small promontory by Freshwater Steps. A fifty-foot well beneath a dome-shaped pump-house taps brine; a manservant once used to turn the big wheel inside to pump piped water up the valley to the house and the bath in which Lord Eldon performed ablutions and indoor sea-bathing simultaneously.

HOUNS-TOUT AND CHAPMAN'S POOL

The gamekeeper showed me these and many other Encombe curiosities. In 1906 Frederick Treves could not describe them because the valley had been closed 'owing to the atrocious conduct of the trippers'. Now, Encombe has an open day once a year. At other times the best view, a glorious and unfolding prospect, is from Westhill whose long arm thrusts seawards. Houns-tout is its clenched fist: knuckles of Portland Stone resting on Portland Sand above the undercliff of Kimmeridge clay tumbling to Egmont Point.

Lord Eldon once cut a romantic drive, under the cliffs, from his valley towards Chapman's Pool, but falls soon blocked and carried it away. From Houns-tout the Pool looks a grim semi-circular cove. The slightest sun turns it turquoise, but strong light is needed to wake the blue tones in its grey cliffs. However you look at it it's sinister. Smugglers found it easy to dissuade unwelcome visitors. One man, moonlighting, hid shivering as a band of men marched by.

They were not customs men but Roman legionaries, perhaps the same that modern soldiers have seen on Bindon Hill, the same ghostly army that caused the Lawrences of Grange to alert Wareham and London in 1778. Some years ago, a boy claimed he saw them

Chapman's Pool and Emmett's Hill.

here in daylight. His mother could see nothing, and asked him the matter. He described the troops in detail, down to the metal fringes on their tunics. If Chapman's Pool is not haunted, it should be. It haunts the imagination with its odd quality of light in darkness and darkness in light.

It frequently saw traffic in other spirits, though it is said that Irish preventive men on duty here preferred sleep to nocturnal dramas and urged the smugglers (I put it in the politest terms) to go away and land their contraband somewhere else. Where the Pool's short-lived lifeboat station stood in the last century, fishermen's huts squat now with boats and lobster pots below the natural battlements of Emmett's Hill. Down there, in sunshine, life is beautiful.

UPLANDS AND DEEP HOLES

KINGSTON

The walk to Kingston is sufficient to work up a modest thirst which the Scott Arms will slake, if you can find it in its shroud of Virginia creeper. The pub exhibits Purbeck stones and ammonites. The beer-garden, with its panorama of Corfe, is the setting for the gravestone of the fictional Michael Henchard, planted there by the film company who made *The Mayor of Casterbridge*.

Kingston is not Casterbridge. It is an estate village, mostly rebuilt in the nineteenth century with olde worlde charm: stone cottages, high pavements, a pump. It boasted Morton Pitt's doomed rope and sail-cloth factory. The first Lord Eldon replaced its decayed twelfth-century chapel with a pedestrian church, now deconsecrated, where he and his wife were interred beneath grandiloquent epitaphs.

As if that wasn't enough Kingston was endowed with another, bigger church of 1880, commissioned from G.E. Street by the third Lord Eldon as a private chapel. A grandiose landmark on the ridge, it stands forever out of place: a tower of eight bells, a rounded apse with a conical roof and a turret criss-crossed with mouldings like a castle out of Grimm. Nonetheless St James' is an exemplary piece of craftmanship, a showcase for the mason's and the marbler's art, a latter-day flourish harking back to Purbeck's medieval glory-days.

MARBLE FARMS

An old quarry at Blashenwell Farm, below Kingston on the south side of the Corfe valley, was re-opened to provide stone for St James'. First mentioned in 955, Blashenwell used to be a substantial settlement, notable for its spring and its deposits of calcareous tufa whose bleaching qualities may have given the well its name: 'Blechenhamwelle'. Uniquely, the acres of tufa also preserved a much

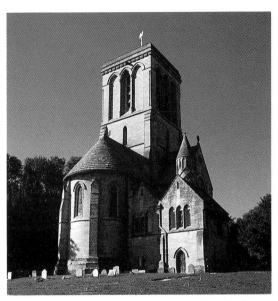

Kingston new church, the marblers' white elephant.

earlier habitation of about 5,000 BC, a Mesolithic flint-working site, which puts both written and landscape history into perspective. The medieval (modern in that context) quarry in Blashenwell's Upper Purbeck beds was worked for Purbeck burr and marble.

If when you think 'marble' you think Italian Carrara, you should know that as early as the Roman period Purbeck marble was used in Dorchester, Chester, Lincoln, Caerwent, Colchester and many other places. Its boom-time came a millenium later. In the twelfth and thirteenth centuries it was employed in countless churches and in every English cathedral but three. If you want to see why, just look at the altar table at Church Knowle; see the pillars and pilasters in the chancel of St Edward's, Corfe, or in the choir at Canterbury; look at the effigy of King John in Worcester cathedral; in London's Temple Church look at pillars and effigies, especially the one thought to honour Heraclius, Patriarch of Jerusalem. It won't surprise you that Purbeck marble was exported to Ireland, Normandy and Italy.

It is not a metamorphic rock, but a hard intractable limestone dense with small freshwater snail shells of the genus *Viviparus* which give it its whorled texture. Two seams of it outcrop at Peveril Point, greenish-grey and red, scoured by the sea, and run the length of Purbeck before reappearing on the north flank of Worbarrow Tout. In between, communities of medieval quarriers dug at what are now isolated farms, lifting out the commonly-used blue-black marble, as well as the red and green and honey-coloured seams.

On a good map you can follow the line of quarries, called 'quarrs' in Purbeck, from Blashenwell to Lynch and ancient Scoles Farm. Further east, Afflington was once large enough for Henry III to grant it a market and a fair. Woodyhyde's quarr was re-opened for the restoration of Temple Church in the 1840s. From Downshay, where the sculptor Mary Spencer Watson has worked for years, Alice de Briwere gave marble in the 1220s for the building of Salisbury cathedral. The farm still called Quarr supplied marble and masons for Winchester cathedral, and Purbeck burr for Corfe castle. Then comes Wilkswood Farm, once the priory and leper hospital of Wilcheswode, whose pits are probably Purbeck's oldest; first-century remains were found there below Celtic fields: sherds, lathe-turned shale, flint tools, iron slag, glass, a bronze dolphin brooch, stone slabs and a piece of sawn and polished marble. Lastly, when Lynch's seams became too deep, Walter Haysom dug marble just west of Swanage Middle School for the restoration of Temple Church following the blitz of 1941.

LANGTON MATRAVERS

From the line of marble farms the limestone rises southwards to a plateau divided, as on Ralph's map of 1585, by old manor boundaries running north-south and made real by a mesh of dry-stone walls that run away to the southern cliffs. It is as if history abandoned the marble seams and moved uphill. From Swanage the eighteenth century turnpike road to Langton Matravers and Kingston switch-backs up to the plateau. Langton lives up to its name, a long town strung out along the spring-line Its fine museum lets us in to the culture of stone, and paths out of the village lead us across the surface of a pocked ground where those with eyes to see can read a long history of mining and quarrying in the Purbeck beds.

Scoles manor house and Downshay Manor, nineteenth century
drawings of two of the 'marble farms'.

Norman's Quarr, Castle View, near Langton Matravers.

QUARR SHAFTS AND STONE BEDS

At Castle View the National Trust have preserved Norman's quarr so that we can begin to appreciate the labour involved in getting stone. Roughly-built quarr huts face each other so that stonecutters could work on stone benches, called bankers, out of the prevailing wind. At the centre of the yard stands an elm capstan with a long spack, or lever, driven round by a donkey to wind up the chain and raise stone from the shaft. The capstan is held between crabstones, supported in turn by buttress-stones. The chain was attached to an elm sled dragged over the slide's crude paving or, as here, a trundle on wheels that ran up the slide's rails. The capstan's ratchet prevented the load running back, and a fistful of grease round its neck and in the gudgeon-hole kept it running smoothly.

The circumference of the capstan, the length of the spack and the strength of the donkey (or men and, occasionally, women) varied to suit the depth and angle of the shaft. Shafts led to lanes, perhaps a hundred feet long, driven into stone beds at different levels. Legs of stones were 'caught' between floor and ceiling for support. It was dark down there, lit by candles stuck in dobs of clay. It was slippery and damp. Humid too, even before men began to work.

Lanes in the Freestone were six feet high, and produced not only Freestone proper, but other seams including grainy Thornback, for which Mount Misery above Wilkswood was famous, buff shelly Wetson Bed and hard Roach that splits for cladding. Beneath, lanes in the Downsvein were only three feet high, cramped as well as deep. Downsvein men, they say, surfaced only in times of dispute. Its seven thin beds went, as Daniel Defoe noted, to pave London's streets, courts and alleys. Locally it was used for tiles or slats, and many cottages are built from its waste. Under it lie twelve feet of intractable fossil oyster or Cinder Bed. Langton quarriers punched or blasted their way through that, or dug under it where it outcrops along the Wares above the cliffs, for the Caps comprising Button, Feather and Cap itself: big creamy blocks that furnished kerb-stones for miles of city streets. Below that again is the New Vein with beds named Sky, Five or Six, Brassey and Tompson.

DANCING LEDGE

Durnford Drove leads out of Langton southwards. It crosses the Priest's Way, a stone-walled track on which the priest of important Worth Matravers walked over the stone plateau to celebrate mass in his chapel at humble Swanage. Then it takes us past Spyway Barn and down to Dancing Ledge. Wonderful names. Magical routes.

Marbled white and chalk-hill blue butterflies dance in the air. Bleached clouds hang in a fathomless sky above the green sea. Dancing Ledge, the quarry shelf above the swell, is hot, rutted by the wheels of man-drawn horn-carts with outcurved shafts that drew Purbeck Portland stone from the caverns in the cliff to be loaded from the ledge onto stone-boats. The swimming pool in the ledge was blasted on the orders of the first headmaster of the first of Langton's many private schools, Durnford House. Where quarrymen had laboured in the darkness and the light, he used to drive the sons of gentlefolk down the Drove to swim above the sea.

The Priest's Way near Blacklands.

SMUGGLING

In darkness contraband landed on the ledge and stored in the cliff quarry was carried up towards Langton. Thomas Hayward, who rented the quarry from Mrs Serrell of Durnford House, was also sexton, parish clerk and warden to the rector. More than once Spyway Farm's bull kept guard over an illicit cache in the barn. Usually the smuggled goods were taken straight to the village. Spirits were decanted from tell-tale barrels, quickly and fragrantly burnt, into English bottles in the King's Arms. Sometimes tubs were hidden in the communicating roof-spaces of Mrs Serrell's cottages. If necessary Hayward took advantage of his position in the church, posted a lookout outside St George's, and had his men heave booty up the tower and secrete it above the nave ceiling.

Perhaps the structure was weakened. The roof of 1828 was found to be unsafe and the whole unsound nave was rebuilt in 1876. That new roof is taller than the squat fifteenth-century tower. Of the church bells two originals survived intact, but two had been cracked by Free Boys, new members of the quarrymen's guild, the Ancient Order of Marblers and Stonecutters of the Isle of Purbeck, who were allowed to strike the bells with their hammers on Shrove Tuesday to announce Kissing Day festivities and the Marblers' annual meeting at Corfe Castle. These boys struck St George's bells with a vengeance.

Maybe they were irreligious. Maybe they were nonconformists who cared for no priest or landlord, but only God and their fellows. Maybe they were schismatics who followed Mrs Serrell when she set up her own school, in opposition to the National school, and her own alternative Anglican services, accompanied by a brass band, which continued in competition with St George's until she died in 1884.

Another fifteenth-century bell, new to the church, was presented in 1973 by Old Durnfordians in memory of the school's founders. A fourth, dated 1602, was brought here from Kingston's old church to commemorate Lord Tovey, responsible for operations that sank the *Bismarck*, Admiral of the Fleet and first Baron Langton Matravers.

QUARRS AND DINOSAURS

North of the road west out of Langton to Gallows Gore the series of pits and quarr-huts – one or two of which seem, by some quirk of planning permission, to have quite outgrown their ostensible purpose – shows that the stone business is thriving. South of the road, Acton was once a quarriers' hamlet pure and simple. It is built over some of its own old lanes and, on two sides, open-cast pits and ridden holes now almost nudge it aside. In 1997, at Keates quarry beside the Priest's Way, the largest set of dinosaur footprints ever found in Britain was uncovered in the White Horse bed. Iguanodon tracks are common enough, especially in the Pink bed of the Roach, but here

A mason squaring building stone at Acton.

are fifty-two prints made by a big sauropod such as Diplodocus or Brachiosaurus in sub-tropical mud 140 million years ago.

Some way west, Tarmac's Swanworth Quarries Ltd. works the massive Sheepsleights pit at Coombe Bottom. It is an artificial canyon, from which colossal quantities of roadstone and hardcore are extracted; a shifting canyon too, for the company is committed to healing the landscape as it goes, though restoration, in the true sense of the word, is impossible. The new landscape must be built with imagination. Blasting the old one shakes Worth Matravers.

I have hinted that Worth was worth something when Swanage was almost nothing. Until 1506 Swanage was a chapelry dependent upon the church of St Nicholas, Worth. There are still clues to Worth's fame. The pub is called The Square and Compass, after tools of a mason's trade. Out of season, at its narrow bar, before its fire or in its stony nooks and crannies you can still hear talk of the sea and the cliff-stone and the men like Billy Winspit who embodied both.

Below the pretty pond which replaced the essential spring, London Row is witness to the stonecutters' links with the capital. The church, whose tower and nave date from about 1100, is a place in which to search out stories and mysteries. Up in the boneyard stand the eloquent headstones of Benjamin Jesty and his wife Elizabeth. He was, we read, 'particularly *noted* for having been the first person (known) that *introduced* the *Cow Pox* by *Inoculation*, and who from his great *strength of mind made the Experiment from* the *(Cow) on* his Wife and two Sons in the Year 1774', the year before Dr Edward Jenner began his celebrated work and twenty-two years before he made vaccination against smallpox respectable.

SEACOMBE AND WINSPIT

Follow the signs to Seacombe where medieval strip-lynchets, or cultivation terraces, frown from the hillside. Down there samphire and sea-aster grow on the cliffs and the breakers thrash beneath ledges. Imagine the labour and dangers involved in hacking out the caverns, or cliff quarries, that gaze hollow-eyed out to sea. Imagine the risks men took lowering stone by gibbet into the boats below.

Purbeck Portland stone is a thicker formation than on Portland itself. The ledges and quarry floors are of the speckled cherty series. Next comes eight or ten feet of good Under Freestone, then the hard Underpicking Cap which had to be blasted away before the Under Freestone could be split with gads – iron pyramids on poles – and got out. Twelve-foot legs were left or built to support the ceilings, and a cavern might grow as deep as two hundred feet. The roof was left, or

Two remarkable photographs of Seacombe quarries in 1932, one showing the cliff workings, the other an underground gallery. Today, there is no trace of any of the buildings.

Overgrown quarry workings at Winspit.

deliberately foundered so that upper layers of stone could be dug out as from a ridden hole.

It is a shame that the National Trust has to fence off the caves. Public liability compels them to do it, for Seacombe is a man-made (or unmade) place which they invite people to visit. I liked it as the quarriers left it, in its state of man-made wildness. The fences spoil and tame a place where men lived with danger and where, if they are foolish enough, people should still be free to kill themselves.

Winspit, over the cliffs, is more atmospheric. Giant rock steps and a honeycomb of tunnels are tempting indeed. The only barred caves are safe houses for mouse-eared and greater horseshoe bats. In 1786 survivors from the wrecked East Indiamen *Halsewell* were glad enough of quarriers' bravery and of a haven in the hacked caverns. Above, second-storey caves were cut for desirable Pond Freestone and some men lived like hermits up there within living memory. The ruined buildings are more recent, for Winspit was worked until the end of the last war. Billy Winspit's cottage, where the quarrier and fisherman lived until he died in 1966, stands in the valley between the terraced slopes of East Man and West Man.

RADAR

Renscombe's masts used to throb and moan in the wind. On high ground west of Worth three wooden towers and clusters of ground installations sprang up in 1940. Here, at the Telecommunications Research Establishment scientists, including Bernard Lovell, worked urgently and secretly on 'the location of enemy aircraft using radio waves'. A landing ground on St Aldhelm's Head was laid out for tests with gliders. A submarine patrolled with conning tower raised to practise U-boat detection. Reg Batt, one of the researchers, wired aluminium sheet to his bicycle and rode about the headland to test the new Centimetre Radar's ability to pick up slow-moving objects.

Robert Cockburn developed technology here which disorientated Luftwaffe pilots by re-transmitting and warping the radio beams they used for flying blind to English targets. Systems were perfected at Worth not only for jamming, interference, airborne interception and submarine detection, but for locating enemy aircraft on charts, and for ground-mapping to enable blind bombing through cloud cover.

ST ALDHELM'S HEAD

At Renscombe the track turns abruptly south for St Aldhelm's Head. Fools and Admiralty charts call it St Alban's, while Ordnance Survey maps let you choose between saints. There is no choice. I love this place in wild weather when the cottages, coastguard look-out and St Aldhelm's chapel seem to crouch beneath the gale, birds are swept inland and storm-tossed Purbeck drives its prow against the slabby Channel. On the last day of August 1997 I hardly stopped to study St Aldhelm's Quarry, where shelves of Shrimp, Spangle and Pond Freestone are systematically dismantled. I pressed on to shelter in the stolid chantry chapel. The doorway's masonry is mined by weather, but in the dim, dank interior the world holds still beneath a vaulted roof supported by eight arches that spring from one thick pier carved with the graffiti of centuries. Girls drop pins into a cavity as a charm towards the man of their dreams. It is a place to say mass for the souls of drowned sailors. A notice announced a service of Celtic

St Aldhelm's Quarry, with St Aldhelm's Chapel and the
coastguard cottages on the skyline.

Christianity that night. I emerged into the warping wind.

Beyond the coastguard's look-out, shivered cliffs dropped sheer to
the undercliff, its skirts laced with foam. On a chert shelf a pillar
carried a crude beaked head, a 'sculpture' in Freestone and Spangle
left over from quarrying. Two giggling lads and a girl clung to rocks,
spread-eagled by the storm beneath the brow. It was not a day to sit
for long on the Head's stone seats. It was hard work walking far
enough to admire Emmett's Hill's crown of stone above Chapman's
Pool's grim clay. On a fine hot day, from Purbeck's southernmost
frontier and look-out, you can watch porpoises or dolphins at play
350 feet below. That August evening I was blown back inland against
the dogged flow of Celtic worshippers.

TO THE OILFIELD

A man who works at St Aldhelm's Quarry is, just now, one of the two Wardens who preside over the Ancient Order of Marblers and Stonecutters of the Isle of Purbeck. Medieval marble exports passed through Corfe Gap and, after a long period when stone went out of Swanage, stone lorries pound through Corfe Castle today. The Order has always convened there for its annual meeting.

Marblers' roads cut across Corfe Common, a telling landscape whose conservation is a hot issue. Graziers exercise rights less intensively than they did, bracken is not harvested and furze cutters no longer cut gorse for bakers' ovens, so men on tractors periodically clear the scrub to cries of protest from bird lovers. But Corfe Common never was a natural landscape. The National Trust is obliged to maintain it (an SSSI) for its turf structure and its wet mires. Those elements are conserved, along with tumuli, hollow ways, ponies and more than thirty species of birds at the last count.

The manor house at the 'marble farm' called Dunshay was built in 1642 by John Dolling. George Dolling heads the signatories of the articles of agreement of the Company of Marblers and Stonecutters dated 3 March 1651. For his holding at Scoles Farm William de Scovill paid the Constable of Corfe a pound of pepper annually.

Roads meet at Scoles Gate and cross the Common, converging with others on West Street. It is said that ten feet of more of 'scars' or stone chippings underlie West Street, for masons dressed stone on their bankers here. For centuries the Ancient Order has met on Shrove Tuesday in the Fox Inn and opposite, in Corfe's tiny Town Hall. From there Free Boys still kick a football over the heath to Ower Passage House, or more recently to Ower Farm, where a pound of pepper is paid for the use of Ower Quay, a venerable port on the southern shore of Poole Harbour.

Heath and Harbour from Dean Hill.

A MYTHICAL WILDERNESS

The tradition has long outlived the trade. The marblers' road is a ghost of its former self, like so many industrial tracks and tramways scored in the heath's skin for the carriage of salt or pottery or clay or stone. There are oil wells at Ower now. They are part of the largest onshore oilfield in Western Europe. It is not rigs, well-heads or pipelines that represent the oil industry's biggest impact on the area, but roads recently built across the heath to service them. If marblers surfaced their road to Ower with limestone from the south, and clay magnates laid chalk ballast from the hills along their tracks, oil men imported hardcore and tarmac in huge quantities. Their roads across the heath will be more difficult to erase. But they will disappear.

Or almost disappear. Heathland is a misunderstood place. Some people would like to see it restored to primeval wilderness. Purbeck's northern half contains the largest remaining tracts of the Dorset heathland so powerfully portrayed by Thomas Hardy as 'Egdon Heath', a wild untameable thing, whose enemy is civilisation. I have my own romantic notion of it, of the very stuff of it, of how parched heathers, heaths and furze, moor and bristle grass grasp a meagre living from flints, gravels and grey sands founded upon an unforgiving iron hardpan; how sphagnum moss, sundews, cotton sedge and bog asphodel flourish in acid bogs and pools. Its fauna excites me: dragonflies and damselflies, rare natterjack toads and all six British reptiles including sand lizards and smooth snakes. Yes, it is wild enough, but we have long understood that heathland is not wilderness; it is man-made, like every other landscape in Purbeck.

Like the whole plundered island, it gains its beauty and, more than that, its poignancy from the tough and delicate balance it has struck with man. Man means us, and our crude or ingenious exploitation of it. Keeping the balance is the issue we must address. Purbeck, like the planet as a whole, is not infinitely compliant. Our generation must not be the one which pushes it beyond what it can bear.

HEATH: A LONG STORY CUT SHORT

Pollen analysis shows that present-day heath used to be covered with dense forests of pine, birch, hazel, elm and oak. Mesolithic hunter-gatherers made their clearings and Neolithic farmers opened up fields. A Bronze Age settlement and field system has been identified near the Corfe river. But cultivation soon exhausted these soils and, by the end of the Bronze Age, about 600 BC, a degraded heathland landscape predominated between the harbour and the hills.

Farmers have always tried to sweeten and cajole marginal land. Heathcroppers, as the peasants who worked the ungrateful ground were called, composed Purbeck's underclass. In the days when the island was defined as a Royal Forest or Warren, deer and hare had more privileges than humans who scratched a dubious living. Smallholdings swelled and contracted before, at last, being extinguished by the land's inexhaustible miserliness.

Without animals to graze it and furze-cutters to harvest it, heath slowly but inexorably reverts to woodland. The process can be hurried. Conifer plantations, managed by the Forestry Commission, Rempstone estate and smaller landowners, have in half a century destroyed more heathland than 2,500 years of human industry.

Scotland Farm of 1665, where the Corfe River cuts through the heath.

ARNE

Of the roads to Arne peninsula the one that runs more or less north from the roundabout near Norden Park and Ride takes us across the railway bridge, though the track will not be reinstated there until the Swanage Railway Co.'s Norden-Swanage stretch is reconnected with the Furzebrook-Wareham mainline. It crosses old clay tramways and skirts Scotland Farm where, exploiting land on the Corfe River's alluvium, Peter Whefen made a better living than most heathcroppers; in Plague year, he built himself a farmhouse with stone filched from recently-slighted Corfe Castle and had 16PW65 roughly carved above the lintel.

Our road traverses farmland now actively being returned to heath. Where dairy cows recently grazed pasture created by years of marling and fertilising the National Trust is putting the process into reverse: nutrient-stripping the fields to speed their transition to acid grassland and heath. As part of the Hartland Way – one element of the web of paths and cycle routes which leisure rather than industry now weaves in Purbeck – a length of Fayle's Tramway has been made into a wheelchair route that leads deep into the heath.

Buried in forestry to the left of the Arne road is another oil well. Onwards, to the right, is an RSPB reserve and nature trail where open ground is ideal for nightjars and gorse scrub sustains a population of rare Dartford Warblers. Hides survey heath and saltmarsh. At Shipstal Point the beach is paved with oyster shells. The harbour's oyster beds were famous in Roman times. Daniel Defoe praised them for their quality and for their pearls, the largest in all England. But Arne's riches are mostly ascetic ones. Its church is a holy barn set a hundred feet up at the heart of the peninsula. St Nicholas of Myra, patron saint of sailors, keeps his eye on Poole harbour's shipping.

WYTCH

Russell Quay shipped out clay from Arne's pits and the quay at Middlebere exported Norden's. The Sharford packhorse bridge seems to link nowhere to nowhere now, but crosses the little Corfe river from Arne into Corfe Castle parish. It meant more when Wytch Quay was also a clay port with a Passage House from which regular ferries carried passengers to and from Poole in the eighteenth century. Today, Wytch Farm is known worldwide, from Azerbaijan to Texas. It has given its name to the Purbeck oilfield.

Early in 1974 oil was struck there at 3,000 feet in the Bridport Sands formation. From Wytch Farm's wellsites a much larger reservoir was tapped four years later at more than 5,000 feet in the Sherwood Sands formation. This would be more than a nodding donkey or two on the cliffs at Kimmeridge. I remember the growing excitement, and the panic among those who feared for Purbeck and Poole Harbour.

Question: How do you develop an oilfield, with reserves now estimated at 440 million barrels, in the heart of a designated Area of Outstanding Natural Beauty with its National Nature Reserves, Sites of Special Scientific Interest, scheduled Ancient Monuments and tracts of Heritage Coast?

Answer: very carefully, with maximum consultation and the will to research and develop cutting-edge technology. BP Exploration and its partners have achieved remarkable success with sensitivity. They put ecologists and archaeologists on the payroll. They have won numerous prestigious environmental awards and are still making advances which will benefit the industry worldwide.

The Wytch Farm Oilfield. Looking east over Wytch Farm Gathering Station towards Poole Harbour and its islands.

Screened by Corsican pine plantations on Wytch Heath, the fifty-acre Gathering Station receives oil from all ten wellsites, including two on Furzey Island. It is processed and pumped along a 56-mile underground pipeline that runs west of Wareham and north of Wimborne before heading east to BP's Hamble Terminal on Southampton Water. Natural gas is also processed at Wytch: methane/ethane is sold to British Gas who pump it to Sopley and the National Gas Grid; liquid butane and propane are stored at Wytch and pumped to the rail terminal at Furzebrook for carriage to BP's LPG (Liquid Petroleum Gas) terminal at Avonmouth. Separated water from the wells, together with seawater sucked from the harbour at Cleavel Point near Ower, is treated and pumped to injection wells to maintain pressure in the reservoir. Liquid petroleum gas too is pumped back into the ground to recover the maximum quantity of oil. Within the Gathering Station, the control room's computers monitor and regulate the whole oilfield. Elaborate warning systems and automated shut-down mechanisms are in place in the event of spillages or blow-outs. But everyone knows that the moment emergency vehicles speed across the heath in earnest, or booms are deployed on the harbour for real, the public relations effort of decades will go straight down the pan.

NEWTON AND GOATHORN

The longest clay tramway stretched diagonally across the heath from Norden to Goathorn Point. Much of the route now runs through plantations that have overtaken Rempstone and Newton Heaths. On

A derelict clay tramway at Newton in the 1970s.

the way it passes Newton itself, an almost-place between Ower and Goathorn. Edward I decreed that a town should be built there, a new port for Purbeck furnished with a harbour, market-place and church (somehow marked on Saxton's map of 1575). The king's charter granted it a twice-weekly market and an annual fair. But the new town – Newton – never happened.

Almost never. Newton's clay pits thrived for just eighty years and briefly it became a community with cottages and a school. The narrow-gauge railway of 1868, on which the Poole locomotive *Tiny* was succeeded by *Thames*, ran to it and continued up the east side of Goathorn peninsula. The place closed down in 1937 when the pits were exhausted. Not long afterwards the army ripped up the rails.

The most obvious landmark on Goathorn today is a 210-foot-tall high-powered drilling rig which will stand over the second multiple wellsite there for some while. As I stood in its shadow talking to one of the men, his pride in the work was obvious. Ten wells have already been drilled down and out, he said, at angles approaching 80 degrees from the vertical, to tap the Sherwood reservoir beneath Poole Bay. The tenth had just broken the world record for extended horizontal reach, at eight kilometres and thirty-seven metres. As I write, the eleventh Goathorn well is nearing the ten kilometre mark.

BRAND'S BAY

From Redhorn Quay you can gaze at the Goathorn rig across the peaceful saltings of Brand's Bay, more properly Brandy Bay because smugglers used to avoid the well-guarded harbour entrance – and play competing Purbeck, Brownsea, Poole and Dorset authorities off against one another – by landing goods at Studland Bay, storing them under seaweed and carrying them overland to Greenland and Goathorn. There they were loaded into flat-bottomed boats and spirited across the harbour. Not long ago a man walking his dog discovered a roughly-covered hole on Studland Beach. You could have dropped a Landrover into it, one of the investigating officers told me. It contained a ton of cannabis.

SANDS AND OLD STONES

STUDLAND BAY

The great curves of glorious sand at Shell Bay and Studland, with
Studland and Godlington Heath behind, comprise the youngest
geological deposits. But in human terms they are old enough to
reveal and conceal much history and many mysteries. On a map of
1721 Little Sea, east of the Ferry Road, was just a tidal inlet in the
sands. By degrees it closed, expanded and was fortified by dunes until
even spring tides could not invade it. Now it is a freshwater lake full
of life.

Towards Shell Bay the beach is gaining sand, towards Redend
Point it is losing it, but on a hot day out of season, when there is
nothing to worry about and the Isle of Wight hovers in haze above
the horizon, Studland Bay is paradise. On a hot day in August we
share it with 25,000 others. Kites weave and shimmer high up. Below,
discreet notices used to warn of danger: 'Beyond this point nudists
may be encountered'. Now they entice us, as in a game park, by
telling us at what distance 'naturists may be seen'.

It is hard to imagine what it was like during the war when every
kind of anti-invasion and invasion device was tested here in secrecy.
King George VI, Churchill, Eisenhower and Montgomery made their
inspections of landing craft and amphibious tanks, and of large-scale
rehearsals for beach landings. Canadian Engineers built Fort Henry
on the cliffs at Studland. The village and beaches were transformed
out of all recognition until, all at once, on the night of 4 June 1944,
the invasion moved to Normandy.

GODLINGSTON HEATH

After the war it took nineteen months to clear away the hardware,
which included 200 unexploded bombs and 84,000 missiles. One

The Agglestone.

supernatural missile survives on the heath behind the salubrious
Knowle House Hotel. From its well-kept garden across the road you
can study Redend Point's lurid sandstone, massive chalk cliffs
petering out at Old Harry Rocks, and specks of sails in the dizzying
blue. But behind the hotel the heath is pocked and lumpy, an uneasy
place where the Agglestone squats on a gravel tump within sight of
the Puckstone, or 'goblin stone'. The name 'Agglestone' probably
derives from *hagolstan*, 'hailstone', or *halig stan*, 'holy stone', but the
story goes, as such stories usually do, that the Devil stood on the Isle
of Wight and flung the 500-ton lump of heathstone at Corfe Castle,
and missed. It stood on its apex like a sinister anvil when I first knew
it, a logan stone that could be rocked, but tipped too far in 1970 and
fell, to the chagrin of Druids who worship there. Holy stone, Devil's
Stone, I like to visit it sometimes, but am always glad to turn my back
on it.

At Rempstone, to the west, a Bronze Age heathstone circle stands in the wood, part of a larger unintelligible structure. Between are many heathland tumuli, burial mounds like shadows of those on the chalk hills. At Dean Hill there are earthworks – fairways, bunkers and greens – where devotees pursue white balls. Enid Blyton lived here when her husband had the golf course for a hobby; the Famous Five gallivanted about these heaths and woods without a doubt.

On the slope of Woodhouse Hill a substantial British settlement spanned the Roman period and got a living from cottage industries, smallholdings, and the Celtic fields on Ballard Down. Today the National Trust has farm agreements which will restore chalk grassland up there to its 'unimproved' state. Hedgerows are being reinstated according to Treswell's 1585 survey. There's nothing the Trust can do about the estate on the hillside. It was glebe land, sold off by the Church. Mr Bankes wanted it kept as downland, but a delayed train made his agent ten minutes late for the auction.

Landscapes are palimpsests: ancient parchments with marks of all ages scratched and scribbled one on top of another; some, ancient and modern, are legible; more are in a language we no longer understand; most are obliterated.

ST NICHOLAS, STUDLAND

We have a lot for which to thank the late Mr Bankes. He turned down Billy Butlin's offer of £2 million for a Holiday Camp site at Studland. He did not proceed with his own family's plans to turn Studland into a watering place. He left things as they were, maybe for too long, until he left everything to the National Trust whose attempts to bring tenancy agreements and conservation measures up to date have sometimes met with no little hostility.

Not everyone will agree with me, but I think that Studland's church of St Nicholas is the most exciting building in Purbeck. Often described as Norman, its heathstone is just pre-Conquest with ancient work (what Danish raiders left) of the Saxon building which

The church of St Nicholas, Studland.

St Aldhelm may have founded, knitted into its north wall. Its builders were too ambitious for the foundations and had to leave the tower unfinished, but they, or the Normans who remodelled it, capped the bell-storey with a saddle roof. It has been repeatedly buttressed and underpinned, with good cause, for it has a marvellous interior: vaulted roof, intricate capitals, deeply-cut Norman arches. The *Shell Guide* says: 'In its firmness, gentleness and mystery it is a religious building of great power.' You must discover it, and all the stories whispered by grotesques and beasts' heads within and without, and by gravestones in the boneyard, to the observant ear.

At the junction of what used to be farm tracks a circular block of heathstone, base for the ancient village cross, stood bereft until 1976. Then a plinth of Thornback from Acton was mounted on it, and on that a shaft of Pond Freestone from St Aldhelm's Quarry, carved into a cross by the marbler Treleven Haysom. Its vine entwines medieval symbols; its double helix, icons of 'Spaceship Earth'.

HARD STUFF AND CURIOS

GODLINGSTON GAP

Purbeck's chalk spine, so dramatically broken at Corfe Gap, is breached again at Godlingston. On the slope below Ulwell Down, George Burt, stone magnate, built a reservoir to tap the springline and supply Swanage with water. Above, in 1892, he erected an obelisk on a Bronze Age barrow. It has fallen twice. I have no doubt it looked better in the City of London where Burt found it.

West of the gap a path climbs between Godlington Hill and Round Down up to the view of England that E.M. Forster recommended, the same heights where Thomas Hardy placed his heroine, his feminine alter ego, in *The Hand of Ethelberta*: 'Standing on the top of a giant's grave in this antique land, Ethelberta lifted her eyes to behold two sorts of weather pervading Nature at the same time . . . The ridge along which Ethelberta rode – Nine-Barrow Down by name – divided these two climates like a wall.'

Godlingston Manor.

To the right of the Ulwell-Swanage road stands a brickworks and the stolid stone of Godlingston Manor which, in close competition with Barnston near Church Knowle, is my favourite Purbeck house, built about 1300. It has a solid defensible tower at its west end, as befits the home of castle-builders, smugglers, and Roman Catholic recusants. Close by, the brickworks, that served the Bankes estate for 250 years, exploits a band of ferruginous quartz grit and the red, purple and grey marls of the Wealden Beds in its clay pits to manufacture beautiful bricks in its arched kilns.

SWANAGE

However indigenous brick is, it comes as a shock, after so much limestone, to hit the red-brick settlement of, for instance, Harman's Cross or the Swanage suburbs that sprawl north across the valley behind the beaches and groynes, not to mention the new flood protection scheme, between Ballard Cliff and Peveril Point. Swanage is Hardy's Knollsea. He and Emma moved down from London, and crossed on the boat from Bournemouth, in July 1875. They lived in West End Cottage for ten months while he completed *The Hand of Ethelberta* and kept well away from his family, except for his schoolmistress sisters whom he considered good enough to mix with Emma. 'Knollsea,' he wrote, 'was a seaside village lying snug within two headlands as between a finger and thumb.'

A view of Swanage, and the Bay, from near Peveril Point in 1823.

Swanage at the height of its popularity on a Bank Holiday
weekend in the 1950s.

South of red-brick Swanage, stone-built Swanage clambers on to
the limestone plateau. Fishing boats still work out of it and Hardy
described how the village fell into two factions: fishermen and quarriers. Two individuals had it sewn up though, both masons (and
Freemasons): George Burt and his uncle John Mowlem who founded
the international contractors of that name. Both of them were incor-
rigible snappers-up of unconsidered, but hefty, trifles. Every boat
they sent to London loaded with Purbeck stone seemed to return
with a ballast of every kind of architectural scrap with which they
could enrich the town they loved.

The craziest of these stands north of the grim Mowlem Theatre on
the front. A granite column soars from a base inscribed, 'In com-
memoration of a great naval battle fought with the Danes in Swanage
Bay by Alfred the Great, AD 877. Erected by John Mowlem, AD
1862.' The great battle is almost certainly a myth. Even the *Anglo
Saxon Chronicle* suggests that the 'pirate host' lost 120 ships off
Swanage in a great storm which probably dashed them on Peveril

Ledge. Crazier still, Mowlem acquired bomb-shells dug out of the hulls of ships back from the Crimean War and proudly topped his memorial to the Saxon king with four of the Russian balls.

Don't get me wrong, I love Swanage. I have been in trouble before for laughing at it and calling it a poor man's St Ives. I have seriously explored its history and economy and I know fine painters who have settled here for the quality of its light. However, the artist Paul Nash, writing in *The Architectural Review*, sends it up rotten. He imagines a shipwrecked stranger cast ashore and grasping at a lamp-post on whose base he reads 'St George's, Hanover Square'.

We can follow in his bemused footsteps. Beyond the pier we stare at a clockless clock tower, its spire replaced by an incongruous cupola for spurious religious reasons, that was once a memorial to the Duke of Wellington and a traffic hazard on London Bridge, and is now cramped by Costa-del-Sol-style apartments. Incredulously we spy an awkwardly voluptuous façade of 1670, from the Mercers' Hall in London, grafted on to the nineteenth-century Town Hall. Further up the High Street we stumble upon Purbeck House, built as a residence by George Burt but now a hotel, an almost insoluble puzzle brilliantly put together from raw materials and architectural details gleaned from a dozen London contracts.

Behind the Town Hall there's a grim stone lock-up with an iron-studded door, 'Erected for the Prevention of Vice & Immorality By the Friends of Religion & good Order AD 1803'. It used to stand north of the church and shows how Swanage was in those days: an anarchic town which puritan impulses struggled to check. John Wesley found few persons here 'convinced of sin' in 1774. The cottage he stayed in was destroyed by a bomb in 1941.

Where cafés and amusement arcades are now, the quay was crowded with tall heaps of dressed stone. Men with no cash used to pay for drink and food with stone slabs known as 'Swanage Pennies'. Derricks lowered building stone, flags, tiles, setts, sinks, troughs and pillars into high-wheeled carts in the water drawn by horses that waded out to stone lighters in the bay which ferried the stone to ketches in deep water. The labour involved in all that is unimaginable now. John Mowlem headed the Swanage Pier and Tramway Company which aimed to streamline things. Rails still run beside, and

Swanage Town Hall, or the City of London's Mercers' Hall transplanted.

into the coal depot now called Playland, but did not get much further.

Charles Kingsley wrote of Swanage: 'A pleasanter spot for sea-bathing is not to be found, and all that is wanted to make it famous is houses into which visitors can put their heads for the night.' In 1885 the main-line railway reached the town. Stone was carted direct to the station. A new pier of 1896 was built for paddle-steamers. All this came too late for William Morton Pitt of Encombe who had tried prematurely to create a watering-place at Swanage to rival Weymouth. In 1833, three years before he died, Princess Victoria had stayed in his Manor House Hotel, promptly re-named the Royal Victoria, but Swanage needed the railway and the steamers to bring in the trippers. Amusements swiftly ousted stones. Candyfloss re-placed the hard stuff.

George Burt's Large Globe at Durlston Country Park.

Recently I watched the paddle-steamer *Waverley*, churning water as it left the pier, from a new viewpoint: an amphitheatre in Prince Albert Gardens built of a variety of Purbeck stones carved with fossil-based designs. Its whimsical surrealism suits Swanage exactly, with its stone lectern and a pair of disarticulated Ionic columns from London's Regent Street via the demolished Grosvenor Hotel.

The ground uphill from Swanage was pocked with quarrs and scar-heaps. From Cowleaze to Herston and Gully an enormous small-scale industry undermined the land. Above Peveril Down, Sir Charles Robinson's villa fell into quarr lanes. The end of Alexandra Terrace collapsed above Cowleaze workings. Housing and caravan parks have spread where once I investigated abandoned quarr-huts, shafts

and crabstones and enjoyed the occasional evidence of genuine senti-
ment, as on a surviving memorial near Belle Vue, off the Priest's
Way: 'Beneath this stone lie our mule. She was a faithful creature
drawing up stone from this quarry for 32 years. Died aged 34 years.
Also our little cat named Too Too who followed her master from
this quarry to his home and back for 20 months. R.I.P . . .'

Not far from Anvil Point lighthouse in Durlston Country Park a
quarr has been restored to remind us of hard lives that changed the
face of nearby Swanage and of distant cities for good.

DURLSTON

George Burt was a hard-headed dreamer. In 1864 he bought the
estate that included Durlston Head and planned an idyllic development here complete with houses, shops and a church, a park
furnished with refreshment rooms, tennis courts, terraces, paved
walks, stone seats, carved exhortations and curiosities. He designed
Durlston Castle to defend his reputation as public benefactor.

While this new world was being created, Thomas Hardy, who
called Burt 'the King of Swanage', sat up here with Emma one
evening just after sunset: 'On the left, Durlston Head roaring high
and low like a giant asleep,' he noted in his journal. 'On the right, a
thrush. Above the bird hangs a new moon and a steady planet.'

In 1887 Burt planted the Large Globe below Durlston Castle, sur-
rounded by improving inscriptions. The globe had been carved in
fifteen sections out of forty tons of Portland Stone at Mowlem's
Greenwich yard. From it we can still walk, sheltered by holm oak
and tamarisk, to the Tilly Whim Caves. I used to like exploring the
cliff quarries but, sadly, rock falls closed them in 1978. Last time I
was here hard rain fell and waves detonated below. Upon the quarry
shelf lay a great fragment of rock on which I could clearly read the
words, 'Look round, and read Great Nature's open Book'.

The lively Park Centre, run by Dorset County Council, and the
Park Rangers' interpretative work enable us to do just that. In com-
fort we can watch the main guillemot colony live on screen, and
listen to what sea sounds the hydrophone submerged off Durlston
Head is picking up: dolphins, too, if we are lucky.

THE WAY OUT

SWANAGE RAILWAY COMPANY

Purbeck's first main-line locomotive was drawn by horses up Kingston hill, through Langton and down Steps Hill into Swanage. The line's completion in 1885 changed Purbeck dramatically and for ever. Well, for eighty-six years anyway. In 1972 the line from Wareham to Swanage was closed and the track was lifted. Almost at once enthusiasts got together and began to work to restore it.

Now we can catch a train at Swanage Station and travel back in time by steam, via Herston and Harman's Cross, to Corfe Castle or on as far as Norden where the tracks stop. The company hopes to take the line on to Furzebrook, from which ECC's clay trains and BP's LPG trains already connect with the main line at Wareham.

Even when the track between Norden and Furzebrook is re-laid, there are understandable objections to running steam trains through a liquid petroleum gas terminal. There are tough negotiations with South West Trains and Railtrack to come, but I hope Corfe Castle and Swanage will be reconnected to the network as soon as possible.

The Purbeck Heritage Committee is aiming, to use the buzz words, for sustainable green tourism. In Purbeck 20% of jobs are dependent upon the holiday trade and 4.5 million visitor days bring in more than £90 million per annum. The island begs for invaders to come and see, but not to conquer. It must adamantly resist erosion of its character. Anything, such as the Norden Park and Ride Scheme or the hoped-for Wareham-Swanage line, that reduces the number of cars pressing through it helps.

Opposite page The London & South Western Railway M7 tank
No. 30053, built in 1905, leaving Corfe Castle bound for Swanage
on the restored Swanage Railway.

For now, we must leave Purbeck by road. When Edward, King and Martyr, was disinterred from his miraculous burial place below Corfe Castle, he was taken and buried with little ceremony at Wareham. Later the Earl of Mercia had the uncorrupted body of the murdered king translated to Shaftesbury Abbey with great pomp. His guilty stepmother, Ælfryth, tried to join the procession below Woodbury Hill, but her horse would not move forward one step.

A nineteenth century watercolour of Lady St Mary's before 'restoration'.

Edward was carried to Wareham on the old straight road which we can follow, near enough, today. Peter de Pomfret, the hermit, and his sons were dragged from Corfe to Wareham and back on hurdles for correctly prophesying that King John's reign would not exceed fourteen years. The route bissects the heath and, at tiny Stoborough which was once a borough in its own right, it comes to the floodplain of the Frome and the causeway across it.

The view of Wareham in late sunlight is magnificent. The town's profile, bounded on this side by the Frome, is dominated by Lady St Mary's church whose chapel of Edward the Martyr recalled his brief interrment here. The church used to be balanced, on the west side of town, by the Norman castle. At the much older bridge between the two, the Saxon bishop of Sherborne, St Aldhelm, is supposed to have charmed the natives with songs accompanied by the harp. There, technically, the Isle of Purbeck ends.

Wareham and Lady St Mary's church from across the River Frome.

But Wareham is its gateway. Its main roads make a cross at the centre of the square made by its defences: the Frome and the high earthen walls King Alfred ordered to be built against the Danish invaders. Beside Lady St Mary's, Alfred's daughter Æthelfleda restored the Priory that King Guthrum had razed and its nuns kept a wary eye out for hosts to come, Sweyn's and Canute's, that would be unkind to the town. On May Bank Holiday 1997, twelve thousand people watched archers fire flaming arrows to start the ceremonial burning of a mock-up Viking ship.

Wareham's history is bloody enough. Its walls on the north west are called the Bloody Bank. After Monmouth's abortive rebellion of 1685 an exemplary selection of his followers were hung, drawn and quartered there by order of Judge Jeffreys. But an unsung Wareham hero, Thomas Delacourt, and his two friends lifted the heads of three rebels from spikes on the wooden tower in front of the Town Hall and hid them under his bed. He buried them later in the east walls. Later he met William of Orange at Torbay, went to London with him and stood guard over Chancellor Jeffreys in the Bloody Tower.

After blood, fire. Fires of 1704 and 1742 were rehearsals for the great conflagration of 25 July 1762 which burned down 133 houses. People found refuge in St Martin's small church, high on the walls beside the northern gate. Tradition tells that it lost its roof in the Danish raids, but shepherds found miraculous shelter from the rain here all the same. A wall painting shows St Martin sharing his cloak with a beggar. The church's earliest fabric dates from about 1020, but

St Martin's church on Wareham's north wall.

Eric Kennington's effigy of Lawrence of Arabia in St Martin's, Wareham.

St Aldhelm is said to have founded it in 698, just as he is supposed to have established Studland church, and given his name to a chapel as far south as you can go from here, on St Aldhelm's Head.

The effigy of a twentieth-century knight lies here, carved in Purbeck stone by Eric Kennington. His legs are crossed, ironically, like a Crusader. But he is dressed in the robes of an Arab, his head resting on a camel's saddle, his hand on the pommel of a curved dagger. He is Lawrence of Arabia. He loved this part of Dorset. Why shouldn't he lie at the door by which we leave Purbeck? For this is the exit, across the River Piddle, that leads us from a small, very large island into something called the rest of the world.

FURTHER READING

Arkell, W. J., *Geology of the Country around Weymouth, Swanage, Corfe and Lulworth* (HMSO), 1947

Berkeley, Joan, *Lulworth and the Welds* (Blackmore Press), 1971

Bond, L. M. G., *Tyneham, A Lost Heritage* (Dovecote Press), 1984

Bond, Thomas, *Corfe Castle* (Stanford/Sydenham), 1883

Chacksfield, K. Merle, *Swanage at War* (Swanage Town Council), 1993

Cochrane, C., *Poole Bay and Purbeck* (Friary Press), 1971

Daccombe, M., *Dorset Up Along and Down Along* (Dorset Women's Institute), 1951

Densham, W. & Ogle, J., *The Story of the Congregational Churches of Dorset* (W. Mate & Sons), 1889

Hardy, Thomas, *The Hand of Ethelberta*, 1876

Hardy, William Masters, *Old Swanage, or Purbeck Past and Present* (Dorset County Chronicle), 1908

Hutchins, John, *History & Antiquities of the County of Dorset,* 3rd ed. 1861-73

Hyland, Paul, *Purbeck: The Ingrained Island* (Gollancz), 1978

Kerr, Barbara, *Bound to the Soil* (Baker), 1968

Legg, Rodney, *Purbeck Island* (Dorset Publishing Co), 1972

Lloyd, Rachel, *Dorset Elizabethans* (Murray), 1967

Robinson, C. E., *A Royal Warren, or Picturesque Rambles in the Isle of Purbeck*, 1882

Royal Commission for Historical Monuments, *Dorset, vol ii* (HMSO), 1970

Treves, Frederick, *Highways and Byways in Dorset* (Macmillan), 1906

Wright, Patrick, *The Village that Died for England* (Cape), 1995

ACKNOWLEDGEMENTS

I am grateful for the help and co-operation of many people in the Isle of Purbeck and especially to Alastair Currie and Andy Hill (English China Clays), Lesley Brown (BP), William Wake and Geoff Hann (The National Trust), Bill Trite (Swanage Railway Co.), Maddy Pfaff (Lulworth Cove Heritage Centre), Paul Pinnock and David Greenhalf (Lulworth Estate), Alison Turnock (Purbeck Heritage Officer), Treleven and Sue Haysom, Brian and Carol Graham, Annie Campbell and Sue Davies, and Christoper Chaplin for drawing the map.

Most of the illustrations in this book are taken from the Dovecote Press Collection but I am grateful to the following for allowing the inclusion of illustrations in their possession or for which they hold the copyright. British Geological Survey: pages 28, 49 (both); English China Clays: page 27; Bob Groves: pages 54, 59; Roger Holman: front and back cover, pages 18, 31, 38; M.O.D. (© Crown Copyright): page 16; Royal Commission Historical Monuments (England), (© Crown Copyright): pages 11, 15, 23 (bottom), 74, 77; Sillson Photography/BP Exploration Ltd: page 58; Colin Varndell: copyright page, page 20; Andrew Wright/Swanage Railway: page 73.

The

DISCOVER DORSET

Series of Books

A series of paperback books providing informative illustrated
introductions to Dorset's history, culture and way of life.
The following titles have so far been published.

All the books about Dorset published by The Dovecote Press
are available in bookshops throughout the county,
or in case of difficulty direct from the publishers.
The Dovecote Press Ltd, Stanbridge,
Wimborne, Dorset BH21 4JD
Tel: 01258 840549.